Heart of the Garfish

Kathy Callaway

 University of Pittsburgh Press

Published by the University of Pittsburgh Press, Pittsburgh, Pa. 15260
Copyright © 1982, Kathy Callaway
All rights reserved
Feffer and Simons, Inc., London
Manufactured in the United States of America

Library of Congress Cataloging in Publication Data

Callaway, Kathy, 1943–
    Heart of the garfish.

    (Pitt poetry series)
    I. Title. II. Series.
PS3553.A4234H4   811'.54   81-70217
ISBN 0-8229-3458-2   AACR2
ISBN 0-8229-5338-2 (pbk.)

Acknowledgment is made to the following publications for permission to re-
print some of the poems which appear in this book: *Ploughshares, U.S. 1
Worksheets.* "Heart of the Garfish," "The White Horse, 1950," "The Lodge,"
and "Viva James Dean" first appeared in *The Iowa Review,* © 1979, 1980,
1981 by the University of Iowa. "Black Sabbath," "Rivers and History," and
"Asvamedha" are reprinted from *Antaeus.* "The American Stand-In" first
appeared in *Crazy Horse.* "It Could Start This Way," "Animal Crackers,"
"Stepping Aside," "How to Love Mountains," and "Love in the Western
World" were first published in *The Nation.* "Della's Bus" is reprinted by per-
mission of Boynton/Cook Publishers, Inc.

The writing of these poems was made possible in part with assistance from the
Creative Artists Public Service Program (CAPS) of New York State, and the
P.E.N. Writers' Fund.

HEART
OF THE
GARFISH

Winner of the 1981

Agnes Lynch Starrett

Poetry Prize

*The publication of this book is supported by grants
from the National Endowment for the Arts
in Washington, D.C., a Federal agency,
and the Pennsylvania Council on the Arts.*

For my family,
and for the Cenedellas

CONTENTS

HEART
OF THE
GARFISH

RIVERS AND HISTORY

It's never America, that place where you
unfolded your fresh body. The town was
always wrong, conspicuous in how it
didn't fit the great notion.

Mine was old Bohemian, not the lost counts
in their coaches, but tillers bound to the design.
After the war those counts married south, their hounds
sleep in piazzas. The redhanded farmers
came here: installed cut isinglass
on parlor doors, plowed their fields carefully
with enormous writing—notes on a stone grade
for orbiting gentry, saying
No one's at home.

Yours was gerrymandered out of Mexico,
a planet of mesquite and gray gilas. You saw
children of Montezuma in the children of Cortez,
in your anguished way you stumbled to embrace them.
The feathered serpent scrolls over the hemisphere.
Never forgetting him, you flood the arroyos and I
run under the river-ice: my brother,
there is no America of the body. We cross these borders
to obliterate the design.

HEART OF THE GARFISH

One thing you don't talk about in Minnesota
is the meaning of water. You can say
what a lake did to you, or
what you got away with in spite of it,
solving that equation where one whole side
equals zero. It's done over beers, at night,
safe from the gravity that keeps us
stupified and turning during the day.
A lake's the lowest thing around,
filling up all the best hiding places.

Our houses keep their backs to it.
We drift down anyway, push out in our
thin ribbed boats, oars beating away
at the surface. We know that underneath is
freedom from the body. It's why we're here.
We push bait on like penitents for the garfish,
because they never die, because we're
full of love. The shoreline turns hourly—
our local zodiac, shapes we live by
when we're out of this.

So when someone goes under we can guess
what he's got: the bottoms of our boats
and things overboard, shouts and blear faces,
inner tubes, apologies, all we have. He'll have
the lifesaver of the sun wholly dissolving,
and years of regrets, like two stones tapping
under water. We'll wrap him in white, for everyone.
He's everybody's. That's why we're back the next day
rocking over water, jamming worms on hooks *kyrie eleison,*
pulling the living teeth out of the lake.

CHICOPEE ARMY/AIR FORCE BASE, 1943

For two days I waved my left foot
out of you, "Testing,"
you said, "this alien place."
In your room at the wooden hospital
the ether killed those roses
in an hour. You had no visitors—
everyone, even the half-born,
under quarantine.

Pale barracks and quonset huts
under a clotted sky—the metal posts
on your bed painted cream-over-green.
You held them with your thin hands
when the P-38's came over,
"so low, so loud,"
trying out air, showing their
teeth for you. Father dipped wings
at your window. You went under
again and again.

I came quietly in the end, not a sound
for days. *Brain damage,* you thought,
but it was circumspection: I had
one leg older than the other.
On the eleventh day he came for us.
He carried me out "like a pale blue egg
against his uniform." In the officers' quarters,
when it was clear your breasts
were not for me—father's metal geese
leaving for China—
I put my foot down and howled.

DELLA'S BUS

We're lined up in the hollow,
fat paper cut-outs in snowsuits. Trees
scratch black on the rising yellow,
and the other way, it's the not-quite blue
of crows. Deep January. We're waiting for Della,
rocking and squeaking, our lashes stuck together
like starpoints. Breath through red wool
has given us white Valentines for mouths.

At minus forty, the phone lines are
giving up their secrets: words fall straight
into the air. We listen to Mrs. Bluedorn, she's
telling her stitches to the party line—
at the sound of "hysterectomy," we all
parade around on our heels. Mr. Utne drives by
with thumping tires, they're frozen, he waves.
We wonder how long people live.

The lake cracks and booms. Here's Della,
her bus is orange with double headlights.
Only Clara Ring gets on before we do—
she sits at the back, too poor to have friends,
her family has goats, and an outhouse. She
has breasts. We huddle together in the middle rows.
Della frowns in the rearview mirror, and always,
from the back, that pull. It makes us shiver.

THE WHITE HORSE, 1950

In a picture dated nineteen-twenty,
my father's sisters lean
over a field in Meeker County,
spare to the bone
straining to see anything
horizonlike. Bad eyesight,
same as their mother. Worse the vision,
the more God takes over your face.
Aunt Helen, nearly blind,
was wiped clean.

She married a Nebraska farmer
near Dannebrog, which is near
Grand Island. His land was empty,
room for anything, his face God-red
from the sickle of the sky, the good eye
a hole straight through to August.
For years they bent together
over wheat shocks, woozy in color
like illustrated figures
from the Bible.

My summer to visit, their house was
plain, it's paint shriven by wind.
They had spoon-at-a-time Oneida,
dishes with web-fine cracks. And that
door in the ground: a root cellar
for twisters, when the cows
flew around and China boars whirled
on haybales. She said
Don't worry,

he'll bring you home.
So when the sky slapped hard
with it's one hand, the horse
who took only right corners—
his white back oat-fat
for my legs—leaned forward
through rain-tines that spiked
the darkening fields,
oceans tossing in harvest.

PILING UP ROCKS

Consider this map: the alluvial fan
of the midwest's rivers. I can put my
whole hand over them, draw them into my body
vein for vein. It's Egyptian
living here, loving water, testaments,
and the dead (our good radicals, they
line the rivers' shoulders as crows).
We're safe, meaning somehow moral. Not
empty, exactly, but conduits
for the harvest to run through.

This goes to the Museum of Natural
History—they'll leave out all
the weather, which was the truth:

It flattened us like frescoes, our
herds piled one above the other.
Weather, weather: a slap on the prairie,
the dust rolling out for miles—black twisters
nicking the pebble beds, or statewide blizzards
out of the mouths of canyons. If the rivers
stood straight up, brittle, you laid down
not thinking at all. Weather could enter you,
the way spiked rods pulled down lightning,
the planet unravelling.

We'll have to dig root cellars.
When the weather rises, or the times do,
you want to press hard against what's left:
stone in a hole, or other bodies.

FARMING AND DREAMING

This long, bare driveway with trees drawn tight at the end—
shielding something, it always seemed, or pulling away
from the fields. They unpack everywhere, stubble plowed down
for the new year. Farther out is a duck-slough. They
come back faithfully, loving our guns, or some continent
opening out under water. Redwings watch from dried cattails.
My father lived here.

We're driving around in circles past the gouged trees—
going from house to barn, house to barn, like a dog
not choosing, out of love. My father's mother leans
out of the orchard calling *Raymond, Raymond,* with her
anxious blind face and that intelligence, knowing it's
starting again. The visiting relations. We're dangerous as
dropped seed here, and just as visible.

The house is austere, empty, only Grandpa draining lavishly
in an upstairs room. A clock on the way down, a chamber pot
and the catalogs. International Harvester, John Deere, Ward's:
red cómbines climbing diagonals of yellow grain, the people-ads
straight up, faded. They were always candling eggs in the kitchen,
wiping off lime-droppings and straw, with Grandpa
calling softly from that other room.

I hid in the barn, whose ribs were thick and fecund. It
sucked life out of the plain house and gave it back smaller,
cleaner, in eggs, mice, milk. Soft things under the floorboards,
Martins' eggs in rafter corners, and in cities of baled hay,
knots of kittens. Every straw moved, if you waited.
Underneath it all were the cows, carrying the barn on their backs.
They waltzed me around for years.

No, they didn't. The dead are so gone I almost ask for them.
I left before it started. When they folded them away
like quilts, I took up traveling. I didn't want their faces,
the lying down and plowing under, their new bodies
sprouting in the lambent rows. Let there be
only this field and the trees pulling away from it,
no one living here, or stopping to.

CARRIE USHER'S JOURNAL

Her rush to finish it,
twenty scrawled pages in pencil.
You were seven, mother,
watched the uneven loops unfold
on the paper tablet. She wrote with her left hand,
right arm blackening to the shoulder.
In the end she took your name away: *Omah*
she'd called you, from the Sioux
those who go upstream or against the wind.
She was afraid for you. The bare house leaned
into the tamaracks. Wild rice on the lake
bowed down in waves.

To make room for you, her sister
gave away a daughter. You paid for it,
scrubbed everything and tried to be small,
thought about your dead parents, missing pages,
my name is, my name is—
history blowing away like chaff.
You ran to the next house
but there were children in chains there.

For fifty years you checked and rechecked
stone markers. I'm writing to tell you
I have found the journal,
it's stained like an old map, and over the landmass
your mother's writing leans like Conestogas—
clear, windblown, so hopeful—there are cattle
belly-deep in prairie grass,
a Cedar River settlement, Misquakee playmates.
Long wagons north when she was ten, her father
singing, hiding whiskey from his brother.
Their open laughter—

She ran whole summers behind him,
wore the same print dress, hair cropped
to save combing. He called her *Dutchy,* they fished
like the Crow. In winter she walked miles,
feet bound in burlap, taught the blacksmith
to write "horseshoe" and "sled-runner"
under the simple drawings in his tally book.
At sixteen a certified teacher.
She had a vision in a yellow clearing—
kneeling down, she writes, *I thanked God for so
rewarding me.* Her mother waited for her,
hands wrapped in a fading apron.

It ends with her father's wagon mired
on a corduroy road. You can call me
by my own name now, it's *daughter,* the word
falling through these pages like tracks
on a pine-forest floor,
prints disappearing behind the walker.

LUCK

for Roy

He tossed it in the family
like a juggler his oranges—effortlessly,
winking at the hole in the circle.
When he took his seed packets from door to door
at the age of five, the mothers
never refused him. He was a sign.

In the cub scout group (everyone
tumbling on the Saturday lawn) he
shattered the legs of the paper-boned boy
only an accident! only forgetfulness
the two of them fixed like
Argive figures in clay.

One year he found a white horse
in moon-packed burdock across the road.
He led it from house to house but it belonged
to no one. As they stood locked in the bright-
ness of the Farmer's Circle, I believe he saw
the loneliness of neighborhoods.

Now he dives his Cessna
over the long open thigh of the Alaska Range,
not wanting to land. *The damned
luck of it all,* he thinks,
cutting the engine. Tips an iced wing
to see if it will hold.

IT COULD START THIS WAY

In the high north
where the planet flattens,
people can't bury their dead
until spring. When lucky,
they pound boxes around them.
In a bad year, no wood.
The loved ones lie
scattered on the tundra
like accident victims,
waiting for moss to give way,
the peat to soften. In the Anchorage
Museum of Art, under the dark brown
blown-up photograph, you read
"We do not sleep
in such a winter. We think long nights
about their faces, about wind
lifting blankets of caribou."

3-DAY NEW YEAR, SOLDOTNA, ALASKA

Daughter of the last chief
of the Kenai Athabascans,
she's here with her Irish husband,
two grown girls, a son.
My relatives press around them.
Smaller children steal mukluks,
mittens, scarves. Her daughters are tall,
wear black silk over their collarbones.
One is engaged, and has a choker that says "Equal."
The other is handsome as a mare,
leans wholly against the side of my
brother-in-law-by-marriage. A Polaroid whirs.
Her girls are loosely posing in their bodies.
Not one son in either family can read—
dream-faced, lucid hunters,
they will tangle and struggle for hours
in front of the television

Her tribe is rich, incorporated,
negotiates as a separate nation.
She hands out gifts like a diplomat,
black hair steel-blue under the kitchen light.
Her daughters are easing out the door for marijuana.
As we pull around the table someone tells me:
Don't ask about native land-claims.
We drink Prinz Brau, Schnapps, Tia Maria,
laugh at old jokes and at her husband who plays
Mad Pierre. The languid Peninsular children
are home by midnight, and to the tipped glass of the princess
I say, *The land-claims: I want to know.* Her mouth
opening like an osprey's
*My father, my father! The pastel spirit-boats
of the dead—*

The Kenai spun into the Aleutians toward Siberia.
There were whitecaps and Beluga whales,
a circle of wolves, the sun lifting like this
over the hundred-mile river of colorless peaks,
and a thin red line of hunters—
We were having another drink.
The princess' face shone like tungsten because
her father was dead and her children
tumbled under the eye of the satellite-fed television
in bright snow falling.

POLARITY

A father loves him with careful pressure.
The mother stays unfocused, her face
blurred with indefinite pain.
His closest friend is afraid
of the inevitable loss coming, and lovers
open and close like the mouths of angelfish,
their bodies hitting and hitting at the glass.

He wants to break down, or out—
has so much love to account for.
In his own stunned way he's becoming a man.
Then let him cover the ground passionately
with timothy and sedge and prickly pear,
his own things. He will lie down in these
and think sometimes of the earth
on its heavy pivot: the heart,
the gravity of the manzanita.

THE SLEEPER

I fly in sharp as Mies van der Rohe.
I sit on the old couch at a raucous angle,
toss out reels of the latest information
but they look away, the kingfisher and his wife,
my mother. Outside, a jay is throwing seeds from his feeder.
All around, the pines are black or pure white,
they are there or not there.
Somewhere under ground they lock roots.

Down the road I go to see Cary. He is eighteen now,
still sleeping after all these years. He seems
dark, shocked, frayed like a refugee. I cannot wake him.
In the morning while we open gifts he rises,
wraps slow hands around the body of a twelve-gauge shotgun,
blows himself into the Christmas tree.
Little angel of inadequacy, he is
canonized still shining.

Nothing changes. There are only too many boxes,
hands catching at the tangle of ribbons.
Don't I hear cries from the ice forest? See
terror rise like fat quail into the branches,
grief scribble the edge of the field?
No. This death is seasonal, expected.
Lying awake, I hear
the pines boom all night long.

PAINTER OF UNCERTAIN GRAVITY

Nothing wrong all winter
except a terror at street corners.
When the light pulled everyone across
she'd sink at the heel of the bewildering tide,
unable to articulate her failure.
She thought the cement
interfered with gravity,
or when the planet rolled over
that it left some people behind.

Friends gave her a bus ticket
and waved goodbye—one box of Dr. Martin's Dyes,
a canister of brushes, watermarked paper
in a roll. She descended at the first forest,
rented a cabin which she would not leave.
Spring came, then summer: she could tell
by the rising night noise,
the violence of elderly neighbors, bindweed
and nightjars, Victorian endpaper moths.

She slept by day, painted at night—
the poltergeist hurling a chair at her,
starnosed shrews and the ribbons of heat
that undulated just outside her window.
She imagined the rage of the old couple
as a cube of pale intensity bleaching the trees—
no color on no color, really,
a delicate business she wept over.
By August her despair had become weather.

They'd left it on the table for her.
When the sun was parallel to the beams
she found the fluted cymling squash
—small, hatlike, water-green,
from which all light emanated and beat for hours
as if it were her own. It was her own. Here was
how she could live then: with the weight of this
synchronization anchoring her
to the idea of the seed it contained.

STAPLE SUPPLIES

An early morning waterfront cafe, the cheap kind.
There are ten red stools to my left, tops split open
like ruptured fungi. I'm still up, chain-smoking and
shaking a little, curing puerperal fever with a hangover.
This is Duluth, so the man on my right is old,
has a gutted face, is talking. He's a trapper,
his words articulate as pine cones, about the woods
on a morning like this. They'll never tell you about
steel teeth set along a backline, as if trap, trapper
and crushed bone were the same where they come together,
unremarkable as ice. Instead it's
Silver Bay before strip mining came, winter deer
peeling the tamaracks like oranges, or picking their way
around solid falls. The white breath of a whole herd
unmoving at forty below—he's seen that.
I'm thinking, *you could die from it.*

City of termini. Russian ships sucking the wheat up,
Chevies to Chicago, fat with heroin. An Air Force base,
a full range of loners, freethinkers, drunks and whores.
End of the Iron Barons and vast stone mansions over the shore;
the junk of failed lines piles up across the river
in the warehouse of St. Vincent de Paul. I've picked through
crutches and steamer trunks, shattered wire glasses,
doughboy twills and the high arched backs of
wooden dress-forms. Found family portraits
stiff with presentation, sepia pouring away from the eyes,
hook-fierce, which say *mark us: a life.* Their machines
that couldn't break rock or save anybody, and all those books—
Hudson's *Green Mansions* where Rima fused with the forest bark
and even once, a Klan romance, a hooded knight on the cover
surrounded, impossibly, by morning glory.

The sun is on the counter. The wing of a fly
is lifting showing us all we need that morning—
a little roadmap in, or out. The old man's still talking
and I ache somewhere in general. He's handing me something,
a jar. It's starter, he says, bread starter, remains of a
two-hundred-year-old batch, *I'm giving it to you lady.*
Duluth, iron city, rust heaps and slag-lives at the wingtip
of Lake Superior—I know I'll have to throw it away
to be consistent. Forty below. Outside going up the hill,
I watch the crystals fall with each breath given.
At the top I turn facing the lake and see
white straight out for miles, sundogs in all directions,
and out of the deep blue fissures in the bay
already the steam columns are rising. They're
fixed sixty feet in the air, all day, all day,
towers of clarity, etchings with no ink
and I'm leaning, pressed whole on the empty air
printing and printing.

THE LODGE

for Ray

He found it on Crow land,
on a lake so big it manufactured weather.
It was shored against the downhill slide
of sand, pines pitched forward
like stricken mercenaries. Brother wanted
something to make whole, something to make his
huge hands happy. He stood among
bushes heavy with blackberries,
watched a white-torqued loon unfold
over the Indian graveyard,
water choppy with pike to the opposite shore.

He threw away his accounts, took his
wife out of town, gave up everything
for that sagging building. Two old loggers
helped him jack up the corner,
drive in a forty-foot spruce. They remade the roof,
hammered the rafters for soundness—
the bats, dun-colored, fluttered at each blow,
dying in the fur of old trophies;
sparrows fell down with the chimney soot.

He found a photo between two logs:
Al Capone relaxing in wicker,
the woman on his left
displaying a stringer of bluegills between
perfectly manicured hands.
The old men came back with a homemade
telescope of pipe fittings, so she could
"have the moon better"—
through the soda-bottle lens she saw
one wing obliterate the universe.

That winter, at fifty below—my brother
pounding and pounding at the weather—
she let something go. They became each other
the way a jay appropriates air, or falling temperature
solidifies a lake straight through to the bottom,
all one thing for miles.

ANIMAL CRACKERS

On the runway they pattern up harmless
as hinged cigars. But strapped inside
you count the scarred rivets, burn marks
over the fuselage, beads of condensation
jigging between the portholes
and their safety walls.

The day this armadillo left its factory,
rolled from its tin cathedral empty and immense,
nobody talked about perfection. They'd
soldered her plates on with hairline torches,
but like me mostly thought of duck-blinds or
light in a Woodstock window, missing a seam.

So we all fly. If only each landing
were the same! These screws of fear are
limned on the smallest differences, they
rattle badly a foot above the tarmac. Our
three hundred errors all drop down together,
coming home prey to the welder's daydream.

Like the shell of a dragonfly cast by
a heavy sportsman, we land whimsically,
a little askew, not subject to the line.
Now the piped cantata only sickens.
And the steward in his Mae West, who did his
best five-and-dime demo showing
how to clean up on bad odds.

THE AMERICAN STAND-IN

Houses the same for miles—brick
rolling and dipping on old drover-lanes,
roofs snipped by scissors
a block at a time. On Huddleston Road
his house is empty. I'm
his first boarder, recommended
to replace Amanda.

He has a long horse face, five cats,
her great-aunt's furniture in every room.
He lives in the parlor with his
dirty laundry, the green velvet curtains
drawn tight. They pull dampness up
from the plaster-roots, walls going down
to Londinium—

I can have any room. He says
"the white cat's deaf for miles"
and shuts the door. Upstairs
I push highboys around, find secrets
in the great carved drawers. I unfurl
out the window a thirty-foot carpet
of fleur-de-lis, making a lawn

Louis Quinze out of his burdock.
I plaster and paint. In the kitchen
I scour his dented kettle, the only one
that wasn't Amanda's. He's leaving
for the pub with his muffler flying.
He doesn't want to talk: he wants
a draft or two.

I can see my breath in the darkness—
fall asleep and dream of wild herds, their
hooves over cobblestone. Before it's light
I'm kneeling at the window and
through the corona of orange around the street lamp
a hundred horses canter without riders,
the Queen's horses, blowing fog,
turning the spokes of the city-wheel.

STEPPING ASIDE

These five Druid cattle
left bounding in a Yorkshire field
—longhorned, shagged,
unreasonable—have outlived
their religion, long divisions
not coming out even, or seeds.
They've learned to start over
without us.

Alexander's captains
backing away from Taxila
found Neanderthals on the banks
of the Tomeros, who slit fish
with long fingernails, gaped
at retreating Macedonians—
that spectacle of history
they turned their backs on.

They're here off Hokkaido now,
bunched in shallow water, beetling
over their fishnets. They cherish bears
for no good reason and forget,
like us, how they got this far.
They will survive us—knowing
there are ways you can
outlast anything.

THE DOLOROSA DROWNS
IN NORMAL BRILLIANCE

Lying on this bench in the airport at Madrid,
I see the opening of Easter, thinking,
supine daybreaks are what the dead have. These
are dark glasses bought last night at Orly
to hide eyes that won't close and a lack of baggage.
A cavernous Spanish liner inches slowly past,
slow as the tiny man in earphones
who waves and waves, his pinlight writing
some new interpretation of safety.
They waver together in the rose mirage.

Over me lean *Guardia Civil* in vast hats,
their lead-lined capes draped unnaturally.
One bends down and lifts my glasses.
Oh I know, my eyes by now are puffed
like adders, gorged royal on this holy day.
There is staring, conferring, uncertainty.
Passport? Ticket? I'm sliding backward
over Goya's plain to Meknes,
pulled like the horizontal bronze Hermaphrodite
whose shock lies flat against the Prado wall.

It didn't happen on Spanish soil.
They walk away like history, asking only
that I try to rise up whole. This is no morning
for rejoicing. Raises a day like any other,
light again in that same relentless hierarchy,
coronation of the usual in right order.
I lie quiet as a bird shot over sanctuary,
who won't be dying, thinking, *it is enough.*
Dancing outside in red jet exhaust,
the little man waves and waves.

"JUST SO" STORIES

Andy drove from Tunis to Tripoli.
He caught the ferry to Palermo,
was taken to Rome. They gave him a year
under the shadow of the Colosseum—
he wrote saying his cellmate
was a Dante scholar.

Dreaming he'd come back like Jonah,
we took a house on the coast in Brittany.
It had three stoves, one for each aspect
of waiting. We ate blood sausages,
bought winter milk from farmers, gathered
mussels in tide pools, half-thinking.

He came overland, obscured behind a Pentax
with a case of pure grain via Geneva.
He didn't want our offerings, not even
the deep red saussiçons hand-forced
by the genius of the Resistance.
He slept with Françoise listlessly.

On the beach we ran circles for him,
naked for his fifty millimeter lens.
We didn't know how not to, over and over.
Cormorants pierced waves for him,
the sea exposed her long thigh twice a day.
He shuttered down his enormous eye.

Once I had him alone, driving fast
to the next town at dusk. We dropped down a curve
just so: light unforgettable, the pink of history,
moss pulled down like eyelids over the houses.
Then it was gone. On the way back it was
still gone.

The last day, sent to chip dinner off tide-rocks,
we saw a skindiver come out of the sea
like a stricken dancer. He gave us two urchins,
we tapped open the shells with pebbles
and ate the sweet pearl-pink
just so. Andy,

of Maryanne-back-in-the-States fame, of
leaping-with-black-drummers fame in the j'ma
el F'naad of Marrakesh, *nel mezzo del camin* in camera.
I have the photographs: an old one
of you caught in the air, another of you
kneeling on the beach near St. Malo.

VIVA JAMES DEAN

Phillipe flew out of Paris, cursing,
in his black leather jacket
his one-eyed aviator glasses—
chasing a Dutch odalisque, his *amazone*
all the way to Sudan. He cried
over the Nubian desert,
sold her for kief and calvas
in the j'ma of Khartoum (arguing Céline
with the Blue Nile dealer).

He threatened Françoise
with suicide in the Trocadero,
his scarf
billowing out the seventh-floor window—
things had gone badly, *crapule!*
He was coaxed back in with hashish;
sold all her books, Algerian rugs,
her jewelry. Not to say
Phillipe was no good, for one day

out of the blue,
under the fists of an enraged lover
he wrapped me in his jacket,
flew me out of Paris
with a bottle of scotch for good measure.
Which only goes to show, hoopla!
That something must live
wherever the heart flourishes.

BLACK SABBATH

She was Frankie Halloween to us in Paris,
but in Angers, Françoise—historically raised
in Nantes petit point, next to the dead aunts and their
ponderous credenzas. To her twelfth year
she summered on Belle Isle. She remembers the women,
black taffeta and apple faces blown severely sideways,
preserved by their stiff lace crowns from
scudding into the Bay of Gascogne.
It hasn't saved her.

Not that she drowned: today I'm going out to see her.
The letter said, "Come, I'm better now. I make omelettes
for a Restaurant de Santé." The train tootles south
from Paris, full of uncles and mahogany,
stopping in a town that smells like cocoa.
Here is Françoise on the varnished platform,
she wears a cummerbund like the infant Juan Carlos
de Goya, kisses either cheek, saying she'll
never be allowed to leave.

The train goes *scree*. We're in a red pony cart
that reads "Good Health" in yellow letters,
sitting face to face in the clatter.
It tips us out at the doorstep, but no one's here.
Only this great stone maw with soot-hooks
and a coterie of peacocks out the halfdoor,
guineafowl and low-slung geese, Françoise
shattering their eggs like heresies.

THE FURTIVE TRANSLATION OF ST. FOY

—martyred at Agen, Gaul, 286 A.D.

I

At twelve I knew enough to refuse
Maximian's likeness.
They tossed me on the griddle
like a white-floured crêpe,
all the townsmen of Agen
leaning forward in a mass to see.
The black smoke spired over Aquitania—
When the angel (or a cloud)
fell on my nakedness, the enraged centurion
severed me half from whole.

People of Agen, you adored me!,
stroked me in the sepulcher
for miraculous cures. The twisted limbs,
the mawed faces—none I minded.
But when bloody Dadon of Conques
founded his hermitage, he sent that monk
as a spy. *Breast of Alabaster*
he called me the first week, then
St. Bone and *Salvation of Conques.*
The tenth day he took my skull to Dadon.

The air, the black light on the road to Conques,
the monk's blood pounding in my temple-bone!

II

They have carved me a window
in a belly of yew wood, added
the gold head of a Roman
and two arms, fingers pinched to hold
stems of the amaryllis. Centuries of queens
brought earrings, cabochon gems. To my right,
three hairs from the head of the Virgin Mary.
On my left the cord and foreskin
of Christ Our Master, and the maimed
ballooned at the glass for a thousand years.

I held bloodroot for the Hundred Years' War,
rue for the Huguenots, horse parsley
for the thud of the Revolution.
Once they carried me about holding
fecund sprigs of rye. My neck is arched
unnaturally now, the gems are gone, and still
the silly crawl up the ravine toward Conques
to look in the window at me.
I'm sick of the miracles, sick of love.
Let them have what they've always wanted,
On y soit qui mal y pense
the triumph of loss,
the perfection of a death at the wrong time.

LETTER FROM PARIS

Françoise, raised on Latin and manners,
gave me her jaundiced lover.
She then drove all three of us
into the side of a postal van,
taking him back again. So they
rode all winter, forcing their horses
sideways up the bitter coast of Brittany.

In the spring she left for Tunis,
joined a Lombard circus on the way—
little Thomás, her son, beating the drum.
Gone for years. Years of the horses.

Those who move overland saw her,
they said, in Delhi, asleep
or not speaking, it wasn't clear—
or fed by the beggars on Goa,
who spoke of her shorn head and bowl.
She was carried back to Paris,
writes from her white bed saying
the road and no guide is all.

TAMIL NAD'

Here in the empty music room
of the Maharani's summer palace
I have slept all day on a plank of mahogany,
wrapped in the odor of frangipani and columbine.
Blue monkeys tap on the long glass doors
with their spider fingers.
Between the columns of the portico
the watchman stands in flared khaki, his thighs
twists of cinnamon. He faces the Bay of Bengal.
So does the statue, listing in the sand of the garden.
The three of us lean like
figures in a di Chirico painting.
A black stain spreads with the afternoon:
we are listening. We hear heavy water
troubled by cross-tides.

We have gathered on the beach with our shadows —
this armless statue, myself and the peppermint watchman,
glistening candy fishermen
and bleachers of crabs with their eyestalks pointing.
We are watching the cross-tides collide. When the sea
claps hands, sharks fly out of its fingers!
They have been here ever since the war.
When that ship drifted in with its cargo of bodies,
turning in the bay like a Kabuki dancer
in a rainbow robe of fuel oil,
the Mayor of Madras rolled the officers overboard.
Now they rise to the surface with terrible teeth
and we all lean forward
as another old warlord tries to
smile his way back to the vertical.

AŚVAMEDHA

For almost a year, the mare
has grown more perfect in her stanchion,
fetlocks soft, her forehead clear. My father
dreams of a sacrifice. He'll free her soon;
she'll dance the long corridor
of the city come out in silk for her,
cream-colored, riderless, trumpets arced
over the sacred river. For a year his
lancers follow—well back, their banners
a distant field of flowers. They move
when she moves, halting when she
lifts her head to taste sea wind,
lies down under the girdle of Orion.
She doesn't know what borders she
violates, the death she pulls behind her
like a tide. The chained ones accumulate
to one side of the secret army. The last day
two captains approach her, slip the black
hood on, cooing, lead her home
at the head of the captured world.
The long horns blow. The mare's neck
arches excitedly. At the iron gates of the city,
prisoners kneel in waves and the sword not used
since the reign of Aśoka—its sandal-
wood grip, the engraved blade—swings
between the mare and the sun,
blotting the light out, her forehead
thudding at the feet of my father.

MARY, MARY

When I lived on the alley I was
flush with growing things.
I made a garden right away, could feel
lettuce and dill in their two-way stretch,
one arm proliferating downward, the other
fluting open with light. I gave them
everything they wanted.
I was faithful.

The neighborhood on my alley, old toms,
a moon-mad dogpack, berry-drunk
cedar waxwings, all came to see my garden.
And one old man who liked to watch me
preen the aphids at noon. "Things mostly stop
where I go," he said. Each night
he closed the bars in his DeSoto,
keeping us safe, like a clock.

One night I had two visitors. At eight,
a man asking for his friend.
He held his arms out, touched
the screen door with pulley hooks for hands,
ashamed of my fear, an old falling-away.
Together we didn't look
where his hands had been. The garden
was alive behind us.

At midnight, a woman in jodhpurs.
She looked like me, surprised,
held a polished bridle in her right hand,
rosettes embossed on the joinings.
We stood there: I was happy.
"Wrong house," she said,
the horse between us missing,
my garden growing.

HOW TO LOVE MOUNTAINS

Not the Bernese Oberlands,
no Grüssgotts here or shagged cows
raking chamomile, pushing moss aside
to drink from carved troughs. Not Wales,
with its stunned sheep and quarried eyes
watching the thread of climbers
over Llandudno.

This is the country of the sad bears,
the stone bowl around Missoula, where ticks
wait days to drop on any heart. Bears,
shoulders rippling, descend the clawed rim
dancing. See how they lie down with you,
flanks smelling of pitch, breath sunny
from the rape of hives.

We give them new apples, make hollows
of our bodies. They line us with damp leaves
from the old life, they'll never go back.
Know them by a litter of seeds,
by the need to pull things over you:
the slowed, internal beat
of their arrival.

LOVE IN THE WESTERN WORLD

Think of family, Ulster Irish
run out on a ram's horn,
our first real move.
The same square hands
ploughing through Missouri
and Iowa and Minnesota,
where we learned to muffle
the cavities of the body,
batten the heart down
on loneliness. Still it beats
family, family, as if the pulse
of our one-to-a-body rivers
ever ran singular. And if nothing
continues—the body ending
in this fist, everything short
of the mark—what do we want?
Don't give me history. No bridges
from my heart to your heart
to all of them stringing back
like dark berries: only
open my hand, press it
for the feel of the river,
the old fishline unreeling again.

PETER PAN
AT THE SCHOOL FOR SPECIAL ED.

They can see right through you,
that's what she says.
"They love without question."
She leans over her recipe
while we mimic their distorted faces,
their long moony vowels, making her laugh.
Where do you go, mother?
"To show my dull ones how to get on."
Father's in the basement
with his bait and tackle. His words:
no sting, no cure.

Make your bed carefully,
pull a zipper so, don't rush
to hold the stranger you suddenly want,
you will frighten him—she says
only small things ever need teaching.
Forty miles to her school
past the factories of Savage and Shakopee,
the ridge overlooking the Minnesota.
This entire valley a river once
—overfull, ice-blue, racing—
no human life here at all.

Elsewhere, the impress of a foot in solid stone.
Handprints on Dordogne cave walls,
and in Savannah-grass that once covered
the whole of North Africa, a man
turned around completely and loved all he saw.
What question was there to ask? No language,
only a restlessness, prints crisscrossing
the shift of flesh and continents, wearing deep
into physical canyons—mother said
her students could never sit still,
never forgot what they learned.

She's in a cast-shot of the school's
Peter Pan. An enraptured Captain Hook
looms over her; Wendy looks sly,
and the star in green rags
weeps with a loneliness he cannot put to words.
A giant, a mongoloid, an autistic in camouflage—
mother's in the middle, holding hands
as if love and connection might be willed.
A stubborn look to her eye.
Never mind history, it says.
Here we all are.

PITT POETRY SERIES
Ed Ochester, General Editor